Afternoon Tea can be a time
for reflection, gossip and scandal!

Display your best china and
entertain your friends using these
traditional recipes ... you will be renowned
for your refined hospitality!

RECIPES
for an
ENGLISH TEA

Copper Beech Publishing

Published in Great Britain by
Copper Beech Publishing Ltd
© Copper Beech Publishing Ltd 1998

Editor Jan Barnes

ISBN 1 898617 22-8

A CIP catalogue record for this book is available from the
British Library.

Copper Beech Publishing Ltd
P O Box 159 East Grinstead
Sussex England RH19 4FS

Tea, though ridiculed by those who are naturally coarse in their nervous sensibilities ... will always be the favourite beverage of the intellectual.

Thomas de Quincey 1785-1859

Recipe for a Good Pot of Tea

There are servants who can be trusted to make good tea. They are extremely rare, very much more rare than those who can make good coffee. The ideal hostess makes tea herself in the drawing-room.

A table is equipped with spirit-lamp and shining kettle of silver, aluminium, brass or copper and dainty caddie, all laid ready upon a teacloth as fine and as elaborately embroidered as may suit the taste and means of the household.

It gives a hostess a feeling of perfect confidence to see this table laid in readiness and to note that the preparations are complete, even to the little silver strainer which prevents the leaves from entering the cups.

Recipe for a Good Pot of Tea

At such tables there are three or four infuse spoons for the use of those who like tea made in the cup.

When the hostess makes tea with her own hands (it is impossible in the case of a large party of friends) she usually has two tea pots at hand, so that she may make a fresh brew when there are new arrivals.

The maid takes the discarded tea pot away, and then returns it, ready for use when its turn comes round again.

Weights and Measures for Cooks

Butter, soft (size of an egg) ... 1 oz

Butter 2 tea cups .... 1 lb

Flour 1 tablespoon(heaped) ... 1 oz

Sugar, brown 1 tablespoon .... 1 oz

Sugar, 2 tea cups (heaped) ..... 1 lb

4 teaspoons .... 1 tablespoon

25 grams .... 1 oz

450 grams .... 1 lb

54 English gallons .... 1 hogshead

English half pint .... 10 fl. oz

American half pint .... 8 fl oz

INCOME AND WAGES TABLE.

Per Year		Per Mth.		Per Wk.		Per Day.		Per Year.		Per Month.			Per Week		Per Day.	
£	s.	s.	d.	s.	d.	s.	d.	£	s.	£	s.	d.	s.	d.	s.	d.
1	0	1	8	0	4½	0	0¾	8	10	0	14	2	3	3¼	0	5½
1	10	2	6	0	7	0	1	9	0	0	15	0	3	5¼	0	6
2	0	3	4	0	9	0	1¼	10	0	0	16	8	3	10¼	0	6½
2	10	4	2	0	11½	0	1¾	11	0	0	18	4	4	2¾	0	7¼
3	0	5	0	1	1¾	0	2	12	0	1	0	0	4	7½	0	8
3	10	5	10	1	4¼	0	2¼	13	0	1	1	8	5	0	0	8½
4	0	6	8	1	6½	0	2¾	14	0	1	3	4	5	4½	0	9¼
4	10	7	6	1	8¾	0	3	15	0	1	5	0	5	9¼	0	9½
5	0	8	4	1	11	0	3¼	16	0	1	6	8	6	1¾	0	10½
5	10	9	2	2	1½	0	3¾	17	0	1	8	4	6	6½	0	11¼
6	0	10	0	2	3¾	0	4	18	0	1	10	0	6	11	0	11¾
6	10	10	10	2	6	0	4¼	19	0	1	11	8	7	3¾	1	0½
7	0	11	8	2	8¼	0	4½	20	0	1	13	4	7	8¼	1	1¼
7	10	12	6	2	10½	0	5	30	0	2	10	0	11	6¾	1	7¾
8	0	13	4	3	1	0	5¼	40	0	3	6	8	15	4½	2	2¼

Sweet sandwiches are also often served at teas. They consist of bread and butter, or thin layers of pastry or sponge cake, spread with jam, jelly or preserved ginger.

DAINTY
SANDWICHES

Using exquisitely thin bread will confirm your refinement to your guests.

Some notes on sandwich-making

The most popular dainty sandwiches are, of course, made of cucumber and cress. These merely consist of buttered bread and a layer of neatly cut, slightly salted green food.

See that the bread is a day old, and use tinned sandwich loaves if possible. Melt the butter to a 'spreadable' consistency, and when the sandwiches are made press them between two plates, with a weight upon the top plate.

Use a very sharp knife, and see that the fancy cutters are sharp. Cut the sandwiches in dainty shapes, and garnish with parsley, cress, etc., and pile on plates decorated with lace papers.

Avoid large slices of meat or any relish as it is difficult for your guests to eat these neatly.

If sandwiches must be kept for some time, wrap them in a damp cloth and place in a tin.

𝒲atercress Sandwiches

Strip the leaves from the stalks, having previously well washed the watercress in several lots of salt and water; sprinkle some buttered bread with grated cheese and arrange the watercress on it. Cover with buttered bread and pile the sandwiches round some watercress, or arrange on folded linen and garnish with sprigs of watercress.

𝒟evilled Shrimp Sandwiches

Take the required number of shelled shrimps, and pound them in a mortar with sufficient butter to make a smooth mixture; add pepper, salt and curry powder to taste. Spread on slices of buttered bread and cut into diamonds.

*S*hrimp Sandwiches

Cut round sandwiches of bread and butter and cress, ornament them on the top side with a border of whipped cream pressed through a bag and pipe, salted and coloured green, and pile up the centre with picked shrimps.

*C*heese Sandwiches

Pound the yolks of three hard-boiled eggs with one ounce of butter, season with cayenne, add some grated cheese and salt, and pound all together. Spread on white bread and butter and cut into shapes. Garnish the sandwiches, some with grated yolk of egg, and some with finely-chopped parsley. The amount of cheese needed will depend on the kind of cheese used; the mixture should be tasted and salt added to taste.

Camembert Cheese Sandwiches

Choose a ripe cheese and beat up the creamy portion; spread on brown bread and cut into pretty shapes.

Sardine Sandwiches

Prepare as many small rounds of bread as there are guests; skin and bone some sardines, flavour with pepper, salt, and cayenne. Add two or three drops of fresh salad oil; mix thoroughly into a paste, pile on the croutons and garnish with a tuft of cress.

Bloater Cream Sandwiches

Cut some brown bread in slices and spread it with the following mixture: About 1 oz of bloater paste, the yolk of one hard-boiled egg; pound together with sufficient butter to form a workable paste. Rub through a sieve and whip in a little stiffly-whipped cream.

Kipper Sandwiches

Pound the cooked meat of a kipper with butter, pepper and salt together with a tiny taste of cayenne. Spread as usual.

Polite Ham Sandwiches

Mince ham, fat and lean together, very finely. Spread some mustard very thinly on some brown bread and butter, cover with ham, press together and cut into small squares.

Grated Ham Sandwiches

Prepare rounds of bread and butter thinly with mustard, and pile thickly with grated ham flavoured with pepper and salt.

Potted Meat Sandwiches

Make of brown or white bread and butter spread with any potted meat. For a change add chopped gherkin or some capers.

Garnishes for Savoury Sandwiches

Chopped truffle, pistachio nut and parsley make pretty decorations for sandwiches. A little of the garnish should be strewed on top of each sandwich.

SCONES
& CRUMPETS

*Piles of home-made scones will soon disappear;
and old cut-glass dishes with dainty conserves
of strawberry, apricot or quince, will be
much in request.*

Crumpets

Ingredients

8 oz flour   1 dessertspoon sugar
½ pint milk (sour best)
¼ teaspoon tartaric acid
¾ teaspoon bicarbonate of soda

Method: Mix dry ingredients with milk, beating till quite smooth. Drop on to hot greased girdle or frying pan. Cook a few minutes on each side.

*S*weet Scones

Ingredients

1 lb flour	3 oz sugar
A little salt	3 oz butter
3 oz currants	½ pint milk

1 teaspoon cream of tartar
½ teaspoon of carbonate of soda

Method: Mix together flour, cream of tartar, carbonate of soda and salt. Then run in the butter, sugar and the same quantity of currants. Mix the whole to a smooth dough, with about half a pint of milk; cut into shapes and brush over with egg. Bake 20–30 minutes.

*D*rop Scones

Ingredients

8 oz flour	1 egg
1 tablespoon sugar	1 teacup sour milk
½ teaspoon tartaric acid	
½ teaspoon bicarbonate of soda	

Method: Mix to a stiff batter and leave mixture to stand for 1-2 hours. Drop on to a well greased hot bakestone or girdle. Bake three minutes on each side.

*W*heatmeal Scones

Ingredients

1½ lb wheatmeal	1 teaspoon salt
3 oz butter	1 teacup milk
1 teacup water	

Method: Rub fat in, then mix to a stiff dough with the liquid. Knead well for ten minutes. Roll out ½ inch thick. Cut up in rounds or squares. Put on hot tin and bake 20-30 minutes.

*T*reacle Scones

Ingredients

1 lb flour	2 teaspoons sugar
½ tablespoon butter	½ teaspoon salt

1 teaspoon bicarbonate soda
2 tablespoons treacle
1 teaspoon cream of tartar
A scant ½ pint of milk

Method Rub butter into dry ingredients. Slightly warm the treacle and add it ot the milk. Sprinkle flour on board. Roll out dough lightly on it. Cut into eight pieces. Bake 20-30 minutes in hot oven.

We had a kettle; we let it leak.
Our not repairing it made it worse
We haven't had any tea for a week.
The bottom is out of the Universe!
Rudyard Kipling

BISCUITS

Small plates should be left ready for those who like to eat biscuits and cakes by the aid of the pretty little knives and forks made expressly for use at tea. Some callers still prefer the saucer only, according to Victorian etiquette.

ℳilk Biscuits

Ingredients

1½ lb flour	8 oz sugar
8 oz butter	A little milk

Method: Mix these ingredients together with a little milk, first rubbing the butter well into the flour, then add the sugar and lastly add the milk, using only just enough to make a paste which will roll out. Cut into shapes and bake on a tin for five minutes in a quick oven.

𝒜lmond Biscuits

Ingredients

8 oz flour	6 oz butter
8 oz almonds (ground)	8 oz sugar
2 eggs	Rind of one lemon

Method: Beat the butter to a cream, add the eggs (well beaten), sugar, ground almonds and flour. Mix all well together, form into small balls and bake in a moderate oven.

*G*inger Biscuits

Ingredients

8 oz flour	4 oz butter
4 oz powdered sugar	3 egg yolks
Ground ginger	

Method: Beat the butter to a cream before the fire, add the flour by degrees, then the sugar and a flavouring of ginger, mix with the well-beaten egg. Drop the mixture on buttered papers, allow for them to spread and bake to a light colour in a slow oven.

*C*araway Biscuits

Ingredients

6 oz flour	4 oz sugar
4 oz butter	caraway seeds
2 small tablespoons of cream	

Method: Mix, roll out thinly and cut into biscuits. Bake in a moderate oven.

*L*ittle Sweet Biscuits

Ingredients

4 oz butter	4 oz flour
4 oz sugar	A few caraway seeds

Method: Cream the butter, mix in the dried seeds, sifted flour and sugar; when thoroughly blended roll out very thin and cut with a wine glass. Bake in a moderate oven on a floured tin; remove when crisp and light brown in colour.

*R*ice Biscuits

Ingredients

4 oz flour	4 oz ground rice
½ teacup milk	3 oz sugar
3 oz butter	
1 small teaspoon baking powder	

Method: Rub butter into flour and rice. Add other ingredients, mixing to stiff paste with milk. Roll out thinly. Cut into rounds and bake 10 minutes.

ℐhortbread

Ingredients

2 oz ground rice	4 oz sugar
8 oz butter (warmed)	1 lb flour

Method: Knead all the ingredients together till they become a stiff paste. Roll out ½ inch thick. Cut into shapes desired. Prick with fork all over. Dust a little sugar on top and bake in slow oven till a golden brown (about 15–20 minutes).

Tea can be sipped at home to cement friendships, can ease a difficult moment and is an excellent reason for an invitation.

CAKES

*Who has not recollections of some
delightful country inn where the honey is
"from our own hives" and the featherweight
sponge-cake is above reproach?*

Useful Hints for Cake Baking

Baking of cakes – Cook in a hot oven for 10 minutes, then in a cooler one. The door should not be opened for half an hour, especially when gingerbread is baking.

Fruit, to clean for cakes – Wash and dry the fruit on a hot plate in the oven with the door open, or in a towel, or rub (without washing) with flour.

Steaming cakes – When making cakes without eggs steam them first. Pour it into a greased tin with greased paper on top and place in a pan of boiling water, with the water halfway up the side of the tin. Steam gently 45 minutes. Then take off greased paper and bake at once in moderate oven for 45 minutes. This process make the cake much lighter and prevents it getting too hard on the top.

ℐewing Meeting Tea Cake

Ingredients

2 lbs flour	8 oz lemon peel
1½ lb butter	4 oz almonds
1½lb sugar	11 eggs
1½lb currants	1 cup of milk
2 teaspoons baking powder	

Method: Beat butter and sugar, then gradually add all other ingredients until well mixed. Bake 2 hours in a moderate oven.

Cakes are lighter if the yolks and whites of eggs are beaten up separately.

*L*ittle Cocoanut Cakes

Ingredients

3 oz butter   3 oz sugar
8 oz desiccated cocoanut
3 eggs
Finely chopped rind of a lemon
1 teaspoon essence of vanilla

Method: Brush some small moulds over with warm butter, then sprinkle them with flour and sugar in equal proportions. Take the butter, beat with a wooden spoon until quite creamy, then add the finely chopped rind of a lemon, sugar, desiccated cocoanut and beat for five or six minutes till the mixture looks quite white. Then add the eggs and one teaspoon of essence of vanilla. Half fill the moulds and bake in a moderately hot oven for about 20 minutes. Turn out on to a coarse wire sieve or pastry rack and leave until cold.

Ice afterwards if desired.

Glengarry Cake

Ingredients

8 oz flour	5 oz butter
5 oz sugar	3 eggs
4 oz sultanas	
2 teaspoons baking powder	

Method: Beat the butter to a cream with the sugar, add the flour, with which the baking powder is mixed, then the sultanas, and mix with the well-beaten eggs. Bake in a moderate oven.

Note   For seed cake use one ounce of seeds, for plain cake half a teaspoonful of essence of lemon or vanilla.

*Y*orkshire Cake

Ingredients

1 egg

Plus its weight in:

flour, butter, ground rice and sugar

1 teaspoonful of baking powder

A very little milk.

Method: Mix all together, spread over two sandwich tins, well buttered and papered, and bake from 10-15 minutes. When cooked, slip them off the tins, spread preserve upon one, and press the second cake gently on the top; then sprinkle with sugar.

*H*ot Tea Cakes without Yeast

Ingredients

1 lb Vienna flour   2 oz butter

8 tablespoons milk   2 eggs

2 teaspoons baking powder

Method: Rub butter in flour and baking powder. Then beat together two eggs and eight tablespoons of milk. Add to the flour and mix into a smooth dough; divide into six cakes and bake in a quick oven for half an hour. Brush the cakes over with the yolk of an egg which has been beaten up with milk and a little powdered sugar when they are nearly cooked. Leave till cold, cut apart, toast, butter and serve.

𝒫arkin

Ingredients

1 lb flour	4 oz butter
2 oz sugar	6 oz treacle
1 egg	½ tablespoon oatmeal

1 tablespoon ground rice

1 teaspoon each of:

bicarbonate of soda, ground ginger, allspice.

Method: Melt treacle and butter together. Add to dry ingredients. Mix well with beaten egg. Put into greased tin and bake one hour in moderate oven.

*S*ally Lunn

Ingredients

½ pint milk   ½ oz butter
½ oz yeast   2 pinches salt
12 oz flour   1 beaten egg
1 pinch sugar

Method

Place milk and butter in a saucepan. When the milk is warm, pour it over the yeast. Mix two pinches of salt with the flour. Add a beaten egg and sugar to the milk and yeast, then stir all lightly into the flour. Grease two or three small round cake tins, pour some of the mixture into each and set them to rise in a warm place for an hour. Then bake in a steady oven for 20-30 minutes. When required for use, cut into thick slices, toast, butter and serve very hot.

Tennis Cake

Ingredients

6 oz butter	8 oz currants
6 oz sifted sugar	8oz sultana raisins
10 oz flour	4 oz mixed peel
4 eggs	6 oz raisins
2 oz blanched almonds	
1 teaspoonful baking powder	

Method: Stone the raisins and chop fine. Beat the butter to a cream, add the sugar, then the eggs (well-beaten), next the flour with the baking powder mixed into it, then the fruit, peel (cut into small pieces) etc. Mix all very well and smooth. Butter some paper, and put it round and at the bottom of a tin mould; add the cake mixture and bake 1½-2 hours in a moderate oven.

Teacup Milk Cake

Ingredients

6 teacups flour	3 teacups sugar
1 teacup butter	2 teacups milk

2 teacups fruit (currants, dates, etc.)

2 teaspoons baking powder

Method: Cream together butter and sugar. Add other ingredients. Mix well. Bake 1½ hours in a moderate oven.

$\mathscr{R}$ice Cake

Ingredients

8 oz flour	1 egg (beaten)
2oz ground rice	½ teacup milk
4 oz butter	Jam
4 oz sugar	½ teaspoon baking powder

Method: Beat sugar and butter to a cream. Add the dry ingredients and egg alternately. Roll out thinly. Cut into rounds and bake 20 minutes. When cold, put jam between.

*M*aids of Honour

Ingredients

4 oz ground rice	1 egg
2 oz sugar	2 oz butter

½ teaspoonful baking powder

Essence to flavour

Method: Mix rice, sugar, and baking powder; cream butter and egg, then mix well together. Line patty-pans with puff pastry, put in a little jam, then a little of the above mixture. Bake in a quick oven.

Useful Notes

Glucose - This can be substituted for sugar in jam-making.

Gooseberries - Gooseberries are good to mix with strawberry jam, because they are cheaper and take off a little of the sweetness of the strawberries.

Rhubarb - Rhubarb is useful for mixing with other fruits because it is cheap and loses its own flavour when mixed with others.

JAMS &
JELLIES

*The following recipes will interest many who are
desirous of making delicious jams, jellies, etc.*

Jam Making

Every cook has her own method for making jam, but inexperienced jam-makers should give their whole attention to the fruit whilst it is boiling. It should boil rapidly the whole time it is on the fire. This will cause any water to evaporate which, if left in, would cause the preserves to become mouldy once potted.

When the jam has been boiling long enough, it will stick to the spoon. The smell will also indicate that it has been sufficiently boiled and moreover, if a little of the jam is put on a cold plate it will quickly set.

When thoroughly boiled, stir any scum off the top and pour the jam into dry, warm jars at once then either cover the jars immediately or leave it until the following day. Tie the covers firmly so as to exclude the air.

The jam will keep for a very long time stored in a cool, dry place.

Apple Jelly

Take about thirty good-sized apples, rub them with a dry cloth, cut them into quarters without peeling them, throw them into cold water slightly acidulated with lemon juice.

When all are cut and ready, put the apples into a large preserving pan, just cover them with cold water, squeeze a lemon into the same to preserve the whiteness of the fruit and boil for twenty-five minutes without stirring.

Pour the mixture into a hair sieve and when the juice has all drained into a basin, strain it through thick muslin, allowing to every 20 fl oz of juice one pound of sugar. Boil this together for fifteen minutes, skimming it carefully when necessary; add some small thin strips of lemon rind, previously boiled in a little water.

Put over the fire to boil till the jelly hangs from the skimmer. It can then be put into pots.

*B*lack Currant Jam

A great fault with this jam is that it is usually too dry, black currants, particularly in dry seasons, being somewhat deficient in juice. This defect can, however, be obviated by using a certain proportion of red currant juice with the black fruit. Allow a pound of sugar to each pound of currants, stir slowly till it boils and take up after boiling for five minutes.

If a cheaper kind of juice than red currant is desired it can be made in the following way: cut some rhubarb without peeling it, put it to stew with a little water and no sugar until soft and it will be found very juicy. Strain away the juice – which should be of a deep pink colour – and measure it.

Allow a pint to every three pounds of fruit, weighed after stripping from the stalks. Boil the fruit and juice together, add the sugar, which should be hot and finish off as for other jams.

Damson Jam

Carefully select the fruit and to each pound allow a pound of ground loaf sugar. Place the sugar with the fruit in a preserving pan and then put on a clear brisk fire. Stir with a wooden spoon until it comes to the boil. Continue boiling for about a quarter of an hour, stirring meanwhile. Afterwards draw it to the side of the fire and after well skimming, pot it.

Plum Jam

1 lb sugar to 1 lb fruit

Simmer fruit till in a pulp (¾ to 1 hour) before adding the sugar. The jam should not be eaten for at least a fortnight.

*M*arrow Jam

8 lbs marrow, peeled and cut up small
8 oz coarse brown sugar
6 lb preserving sugar
2 lemons (rind and juice)
1 pint boiling water
2 oz whole ginger

Boil the water with the brown sugar. Pour over the marrow. Let it stand 2 days. Drain off liquid and put the marrow, preserving sugar, rind and juice of lemons and the ginger (tied in muslin) into preserving pan. Bring to the boil and cook slowly till clear (about 5 hours).

Once stored, jars should never be moved until they are required for use.

*C*herry Jelly

Take two pounds of the cherries and cook gently with a few red currants until the fruit is soft. Squeeze through a flannel bag. Allow one pint of this fruit liquid for every pound of sugar. Stir together until the sugar is dissolved then boil rapidly until the jelly is set.

𝒟ried Apricot Jam

1 lb dried fruit; 4 pints water; 3½ lbs sugar.

Wash and then soak apricots in the water 24 hours. Boil slowly till tender (1 hour). Add sugar. Bring to boil and boil till it sets (half an hour), stirring frequently.

ℛaspberry Cream

Take a pint of raspberries, remove the stalks and cover them with three ounces of powdered sugar. Leave for an hour to draw the juice. Pass the fruit and juice through a fine hair sieve, and pour the juice into a lined saucepan. When hot add three-quarters of an ounce of gelatine which has been soaked in two tablespoons of milk. When it is melted, strain into the sieved fruit, mix all together, and ascertain if a little more sugar is needed. Whip half-a-pint of thick cream, and stir the raspberry mixture (when cold) into it; colour with carmine, whisk for a few minutes, and pour into a wetted mould.

Flowers

For a perfect afternoon tea, not only should the beverage itself be unimpeachable, but the accompaniments should be well chosen, and the surroundings of an order to tempt the appetite by suggesting refined and intelligent arrangements, consequently inspiring perfect confidence in the hostess.

Flowers should be scattered about the room. They must be of course, fresh and dainty. Some people are peculiarly sensitive to the odour of stale water in which flowers have been left for days. Many of us are not as particular as we might be with regard to this point.

Flowers

We are meant to enjoy the fragrance of flowers, but there are women who faint if too long in proximity to such flowers as the tuberose, orange blossom or auratum lily.

The careful hostess, however much she may enjoy these olfactory delights, will see to it that when friends drop in to tea, the blossoms are banished to the background as decoration until she regains her solitude.

Tea water will always keep flowers fresh.

A Recipe for Friendship at a Tea Party

Introductions are not always made at tea-parties; nor always at dinner-parties, for that matter. At the lesser meal the hostess uses her discretion in introducing. Having first made herself acquainted with the wishes of both parties, she introduces two whom she knows to be interested in some particular subject. To introduce casually two persons merely because they happen to be neighbours may be doing an unkindness to both. One may be a busy woman to whom time is money; the other an unoccupied person with unlimited leisure to bestow upon her acquaintance. She may be the type which "won't keep you a moment" and talks without stopping for two hours.

It is much safer to introduce two who live miles apart. They are less likely to become enemies after a year or so of tolerating each other's proximity.

The 'absolutely necessary' Tea Gown

'A loose easy garment ...'

Thoughts of winter will bring forth the subject of the tea gown for, although always delightful and dear to the feminine mind, the tea gown is more welcome than ever in the days of blazing fires and cosy meals by lamplight.

At least one tea-gown is an *absolute necessity* to every woman, for nothing can quite take its place. When coming home from a long walk or a weary round of calls on a cold, dull day, no-one can deny that it is pleasant to think that on reaching home one's tight outdoor costume can be exchanged for a loose, easy garment, in which one can enjoy tea and a chat in front of the fire before dressing for dinner.

Recipes to Remove Stains

Tea spills on linen

Tea stains on gowns or tea linen may be removed by dipping the linen in sour buttermilk and then drying it in a hot sun. Then wash again in cold water and boil the linen till the stain is gone.

Tea stains - another method

When fresh, pour boiling water through the stained portion of the fabric, from a height. If old and dry, soak in glycerine or strong cold borax water for half an hour before treating as above.

Cream

If the tea contained cream, it may be necessary to treat first for grease by rubbing with glycerine or lard, and then to wash with warm water and soap. Obstinate stains can be bleached with permanganate.

Recipes to Remove Stains

Marks from fruit

Any acid fruit stains may be removed by tying some pearlash up in the stained part; scrape some soap in cold soft water and boil the linen till the stain is gone.

Mildew

To take out mildew from table linen, mix some soft soap with powdered starch, half as much salt and the juice of a lemon. Apply it to the cloth with a brush then let it lay on the grass day and night until the stain comes out.

Miscellanea

Metal tea pots

Metal tea pots when not used for some time, frequently have an unpleasantly musty smell and give the tea made in them a distinctly disagreeable taste. To prevent this, place a lump of sugar in the tea pot before putting it away.

Tea stains on china

Stains on china, caused by tea can easily be removed if they are rubbed with damp salt.

To clean copper kettles

To clean copper kettles, rub with lemon or vinegar and salt, wash off with soapy water . Remove any burn marks or smoke marks with silver sand and then polish using a linen rag.

Miscellanea

Tea, To flavour

Keep dried orange peel in the tea canister and add a piece one inch square to each drawing of tea.

Washing dishes which have held milk

Dishes which have held milk should be rinsed out with cold water before placing them in hot water.

Cane Chairs

Tea in the garden is a delight and this hint will ensure that your cane chairs remain as good as new. Turn up the chair bottom and with hot water and a sponge wash the cane-work well, so that it may be well soaked. Should it be dirty you must add soap; let it dry in the air, and you will find it as tight and firm as when new, provided the cane is not broken.

*Copper Beech Gift Books
are designed and printed
in Great Britain.*